Melodies of Morning Light

An Emotional and Mystical Journey through Song

Copyright © Alimentanima Books

Second Edition, 2021

ISBN: 978-0-6450732-5-6

Published by Alimentanima Books, Canberra, Australia

All rights reserved. No part of this publication may be reproduced, transmitted, or stored in a a retrieval system without the written permission of the publisher.

Ink of the Heart

Translations of the songs of P.R. Sarkar

'Prabhát Saṃgiita is the feeling of the heart, and the expression of the heart, and it has been written with the ink of the heart.'

(P.R. Sarkar, 2 January 1983, Ananda Nagar)

CONTENTS

IX	Forward
Pg. 1	Introduction
Pg. 24	Seasons and Nature
Pg. 40	Sadness, Solitude and Melancholy
Pg. 56	Love and Longing
Pg. 76	Ecstasy and Awakening
Pg. 94	Struggle
Pg. 104	Social and Environmental Consciousness
Pg. 114	Notes
Pg. 118	Bibliography

Forward

Words are like icebergs that can reveal different levels of depth. We may choose to cling to their superficial meanings in reference to mundane, daily life. However, by keeping them at this level they become rusty, even meaningless, the more we either distort or ignore their real significance, like a child which says "I'm sorry" just to avoid punishment, instead of reflecting deeply about what "being sorry" means to all the parties involved.

Maybe this is one of the reasons that many of us are blind to the true significance of spiritual poetry. Very often, it uses words which have had their deeper meaning stolen by ritualistic, banal and repetitive use. Words like love, divine, flower, colour, mind and soul become cliché, instead of being doorways to subtler realms of perception of ourselves, the world and the cosmos. Fortunately, there are artists who are capable of crossing through this banalization of spirituality and creating poetry that is so powerful, yet so simple, that we could remain hours contemplating the rich layers of meaning in a single poem, or even of a single word. Poets like Tagore, Rumi, Hafiz, Saint Theresa of Avila, and more recently, Prabhat Rainjan Sarkar- or Anandamurtii, as he is called by his devotees.

Anandamurtii, the founder of the socio-spiritual movement 'Ananda Marga', composed 5018 songs, known as Prabhat Samgiita- 'Songs of the New Dawn.' Putting aside the melodies, which are not the prime source for this book, the lyrics of Anandamurtii are a masterpiece of spiritual philosophy and practice condensed into beautiful metaphors, images and sensory and supra-sensory experiences. Even when we feel that there is repetition of words and themes, it is clear that he is describing subtle tonalities of the mind and heart, just like in Indian classical music, where every slight change of tone by the musicians means a lot and creates a singular emotion. It feels like nothing has changed and, at the same time, everything is different.

Though the musical and poetic universe he created is so immense, it is, still, not easily accessible for many of us. Not only because we sometimes lack concepts and internal experiences that would makes us understand the deeper levels of meaning of what is being said, but also for more mundane reasons: many of the songs were never professionally translated, nor were they analysed in a systematic way, so that even those who are alien to spiritual philosophy could have an initial opening to build their own understanding upon. Most of the songs were composed in Bengali language or other endemic Indian languages. Only a few were originally created in languages that are familiar for us, Westerners, such as English. Since Sarkar's work is not mainstream (still) in the West, and Ananda Marga's community is recent and still growing, the context didn't favour the songs to be professionally translated and interpreted.

That is why this book is such a jewel. In a systematic, poetic and selfless way, Didi Ananda Tapasiddha took to herself the mission to coordinate the translation, along with other collaborators, of some of the various masterpieces of the Prabhat Samgiita collection. Not only that, she has prepared for us an introduction which sheds light on the brilliance of Sarkar's writings and the depth of the philosophy which he has shared with the world. This knowledge was disclosed in a variety of ways: besides his songs, he wrote hundreds of books on different aspects of life, and he was a spiritual leader and social-activist.

To read this book is to open one window of a golden house full of so many more windows and doors. The opening is small, considering the size of the house. However, how much light comes out from there! These are just a few of the thousands of songs Sarkar wrote, that, in turn, are just one of the myriad aspects of his legacy, and Didi Ananda Tapasiddha's perspective is just one out of many possible viewpoints available. Yet, one feels like we could read and re-read this book for years and still be amazed and provoked by the depth of each word, each poem, and each reflection. It is a book for contemplation. No wonder then, that it really feels like silent music, playing within a profound space of our hearts.

Gustavo Prudente
4 February 2019

Introduction

A few years back I began an attempt to re-translate some songs from the collection of 5018 mystical compositions of Prabhat Rainjan Sarkar, known as Prabhat Samgiita, or 'Songs of the New Dawn', with Prabhat being also the first name of the author and thus, in the Indian tradition, the prefix to his collection of songs. It was a humble effort to improve some of the existing translations, which were in rather stilted English, for use among a small group with the intention that their inner meaning and symbolism could be more easily understood. In the process I received encouragement from various sources and began to contemplate more deeply about the purpose of these songs. Parallel to this, I was teaching meditation in Europe and had been observing some peculiar common patterns and also empty spaces in people's understanding and capacity to deal with certain psychological and emotional experiences, which were considered 'problems' rather than natural processes of human growth. The songs of Prabhat Samgiita, on the other hand, touched many angles of human emotion and development, phases of human life, and also the depths of spiritual philosophy and mystical experience in a most natural way, within the context of life as a continuous flow of spiritual discovery and mental expansion. I realised that they had much to teach, and in a very unique way. With this in mind it occurred to me that these songs, in order to be made more easily accessible to the general public, could also be presented as poems and read in much the same way as the compositions of Rabindranath Tagore, Rumi, or Kabir are known in the west.

Of course, the charm of a song lies in its melody and rhythm, and in the emotional flow and voice of the singer, which cannot be captured on paper. The written word, however, has the speciality of giving one the chance to read and reread, and the time to contemplate over the inner meaning of each song, each symbol and each word, especially for those who are unable to understand the original language in which they were written.

The 5018 songs of Prabhat Samgiita were composed within a span of just eight years, from September 14th 1982 until October 20th 1990. Their author, Prabhat Rainjan Sarkar, was also the spiritual guru and founder of Ananda Marga, known to his disciples as Shrii Shrii Anandamurti. Most of the songs were written in Bengali and composed in a great variety of musical styles. Some were also written in Urdu, Hindi, English, Sanskrit, Magathi, Maethili and Angika. My purpose here is to present the poetic and symbolic nature of the songs. The melodies and songs themselves, and information about their musical aspects, can be found elsewhere.

I would like to add that these translations are only a first attempt at a presentation that can be easily read by anyone possessing the interest to do so, and are surely far from perfect. I would be most happy (and in fact it is my hope), that others in future will improve upon and correct them. They are the product of the help of many people, some whose names have now been lost in time. Without the original translations, however uncomfortable their English may have been, these versions would not exist. Many thanks goes to the creator of the Prabhat Samgiita website, who has made the entire collection of 5018 songs available to all, and which I am sure the making of was a tedious task; to Nirukta Bose, who unknowingly encouraged me with some of his word-for-word translations and corrections; and to all who gave me the chance to spend time in India and especially Bengal, allowing me to better understand the natural imagery contained within the songs.

Following is a brief analysis of certain aspects of the songs: symbolic, philosophical and psychological, so that the reader can better place them in their context. Any misinterpretations are mine and I welcome correction, but I hope that I have touched something of their inner spirit. The songs themselves have been divided into six categories for ease of reading, and are not in numerical order. The categories are in no way arbitrary and in most cases overlap.

MYSTICISM IN SONG

Mysticism, as defined by P.R. Sarkar himself, is 'the never-ending endeavour to find the link between the finite and the infinite.'[1] It is the human search to discover the essence and cause of life itself, not only philosophically, but through a transformation of the self, through knowing and becoming that very essence. The God of mystical experience is neither an abstract philosophical one, nor anything concrete. He is the essence of our own hearts, discovered over and over again within each individual. He is formless and yet revealed through the variegated forms of creation: in the changing seasons of nature and the varying emotions of life, in the flow of the river, the singing of birds, in the sky when it is clear and also when stormy, within both pain and joy. He is the 'Maner Manush' or 'Man of the Heart' of Baul tradition, the 'Jiivan Devata', the divinity of life, of Rabindranath Tagore, and the 'Bandhu', the eternal and ever present friend of Prabhat Samgiita.[2]

Song and music on the one hand serve to facilitate the humanising of philosophical ideas so that they break the bonds of intellect and touch the heart, and on the other hand, express intangible experiences better than logic and reason ever can. Music has always served as a powerful tool in lifting the mind from mundane troubles and leading it towards subtler experiences of the self. Through song the sense of transcendent beauty and aesthetics which at times arises spontaneously from within through contact with nature, through art, or human goodness, can be cultivated consciously as a spiritual practice, without the need for any other material except the human body itself. Music is not 'necessary' in any utilitarian sense of the word yet we keep on creating it regardless, thus proving that the needs of humanity are not only material ones.[3] The symbolism of poetry is at once earthy and abstract: a tangential point in which the created world and the infinite, the personal and the universal, human emotion and devotional song, all meet and merge. The 5018 songs of Prabhat Samgiita, if one looks carefully, contain within them the whole spiritual philosophy and metaphysics of their author as propounded in his more formal books and discourses, but perhaps more importantly, you can find guidance and explanations of the internal processes by which an ideal is transformed into a real human experience, through which the claim that 'God is in the heart of all and all is God' can go from being a mere statement to a vibrant, living truth.

In the original Bengali of Prabhat Samgiita, the divine is always referred to with the informal 'you' ('tumi'), and this is done very consciously. One comes to know and love another person through familiarity, intimacy and affection, not though a relationship of power and fear, which create distance. And so too it is with the infinite consciousness reflected within each human being as their atman, or soul.[4] We known Him through loving Him, so much so that this love become union.[5] If Prabhat Samgiita were composed solely to establish this sentiment, and transform the fearful love of the divine (and so too inevitably of ourselves, other human beings and the world), into a fearless love,[6] this alone would justify the effort of writing 5018 songs in little more than eight years.

Here is worth mentioning the philosophical inclination of the author of Prabhat Samgiita: unlike in certain other schools of Indian thought, according to Sarkar, the would cannot be considered as an illusion or an obstacle in the realization of the divine. Put simply it is a 'relative truth' through which a deeper, everlasting truth can be realised.[7] Every expression of life, whether joyful or painful, is pointing towards the same essence. One cannot love God without loving the world, and one loves God through expanding one's empathy until it includes the whole created universe. It is empathy, not indifference, which should be cultivated as a spiritual quality:

'...the individual should feel a fraternal emotion for and attachment to the external world. This sentimental contact with the external world

is a must. If someone is under the impression that 'I am doing sádhana (spiritual practice) for the sake of personal liberation and I have nothing to do with the world,' and thus denies his or her contact with external physicality, although the person's physical body is very much in the world, the person is cheating himself and indulging in selfishness.'[8]

The same has been expressed by the poet Rabindranath Tagore:

'...the highest purpose of this world is not merely living in it, knowing and making use of it, but realizing our own selves in it through expansion of sympathy; not alienating ourselves from it and dominating it, but comprehending and uniting it with ourselves in perfect union.'[9]

One way of developing this sympathy is through song and poetry, a truth which has been discovered by countless mystics throughout the ages, and a tradition which Prabhat Samgiita offers a valuable and as yet not fully understood contribution to.

Before going on, it should be mentioned that in Bengali language, there is only one pronoun for he and she, which is in neuter form, and it is therefore a simple matter to refer to any person or entity without specifying their gender. For the sake of ease of translation, in this book 'He' (capitalised) has been used when referring to the infinite or divine. The capitalised 'You' also refers to the same. Obviously when referring to the formless, infinite consciousness, the question of gender is absurd, and this should therefore be considered as simply a limitation of language with no further implications. The English 'it' quite clearly cannot be used when speaking of intimate personal feelings.

This said, there also exist a variety of devotional traditions in which it is considered fortuitous for the spiritual aspirant, male or female, to symbolically take the feminine bhává (mental flow) upon themselves, and therefore also to sing or write in the voice of a female when approaching God. This is not out of consideration that the divine is in any way masculine, but rather refers to the idea that a woman can more easily surrender her egoistic tendencies and extend her feelings beyond herself.[10] This is a rather subtle and symbolic proposal, not exactly a literal one, and a matter of personal preference. In a similar manner, one may also personify one's relation to the divine through the feeling of love towards a dear friend, beloved, or in some other similar way,[11] with the purpose of creating a sentimental flow that moves the mind forwards, and not, it need be stated, because the infinite is literally any of these things. There is in fact a deep and subtle, and perhaps to large part unconscious, understanding of human psychology at work in the devotional traditions which is well worth examining further. It is within this context that the Indian concept of the spiritual guru, so often misunderstood, including within India itself, can be properly conceptualized. Seeking the infinite which is both within and beyond creation, within and beyond oneself, there is no contradiction in finding it at once in the suspended mind in meditation, the expressive flow of devotional song, in the friction between contrasting emotional states, in the artwork of nature, and in the inner personal relationship to one's guru as an embodiment of the mysterious connection between form and formless. 'He' is to be found in all of these together, as we discover how to use our humanity to ever surpass its own seeming limitations. This is the speciality of mystical and devotional song: instead of denying our human feelings, it takes them and places them in a new context in which they can serve as a catalyst for spiritual growth.

MYSTICISM AND EMOTION

Browsing through the 5018 songs of Prabhat Samgiita, one will quickly notice that they are not all songs of overwhelming happiness or ecstasy, although a great many also are. 5018 songs speaking only about happiness would quite naturally become tiring, and would also be an unrealistic interpretation of human emotion. Yet I have observed, at least in my time teaching meditation in the West, that there is a common predilection towards trying to be 'happy' all the time. An alternative version along the same lines is the attempt to be continuously 'mindful and calm', without the troublesome need to confront deep or strong emotions. Or, in other words, to confront one's own self and the meaning of life in all it colourful forms.

One of my initial reasons for translating these songs was to use them to demonstrate to my meditation students the fact that sadness as much as happiness, desperation and despair as much as joy, are perfectly normal experiences. One could even go so far as to say that depression or deep melancholy are almost necessary stages of life, which most people will have to pass through to some degree or another at some point of time.[12] They are only problems insomuch as life is considered to be a never-ending (and exhausting) search for stimulative pleasure, or as long as we do not have an appropriate context to place them into or tools with which to deal with them. Pain is not a problem in itself, the problem is a lack of greater perspective. Mystical poetry and song serve as a study not only of the human mind, but more importantly, of what to do with it, and of the confirmation that a human being has the capacity to transform his own emotional state. In short, he is not a slave. The mind and its emotions are not a painting completed, but a pallet of paint, with which can be painted many things.

Take for example, song number 4185, which begins by saying:

Morning to evening, I sit in solitude, thinking:
'There is no one in all the three worlds
which I can call my own.
I am alone, completely alone.

I watch the sun rise and set,
the moon as it arrives, smiling,
but they do not stop for me.
I am alone ,completely and utterly alone.

This song is an expression of utter loneliness, which includes within it the feeling of abandonment and the incapacity to be understood by others. Not even the sun and the moon, let alone other human beings, stop to offer their consolation.

The song ends with the reflection:

Who is it that moves the sun?
Who is it that gives the evening moon its smile?
Only that essence will remain eternally.
I desire Him alone,
for Him I sing with all my heart.

These simple lyrics have much to say about the necessity of loneliness as a catalyst for contemplation. Loneliness does not have to mean being physically alone: it is also the sense of being misunderstood, and the honest recognition that there is no other human being who can fully erase this predisposition of the mind. This acceptance brings a certain peace, when it is answered with the offer of a different kind of search, a search for the origin of our sense of separation. When we are able to grasp the essence of loneliness, then only will we be capable of knowing the sensation of union, and to truly give and receive love from others. In the words of the Persian poet Saorabh Sepehri:

'...It is in this loneliness that the overflowing occurs...'[13]

Song 3320 takes the feeling melancholy combined with a sense of betrayal and perhaps also of self-pity, and transforms them into a question:

I called out to You,
I called and called,
why didn't you listen?

My eyes where filled with tears.
Why didn't You respond?

The world deliberately deceives me,
will You also do the same?
Filled with fear, I keep my love hidden
unless it should vanish away.

Why didn't You listen to my ardent calling?

The obvious question, a perfectly valid one, is that did a desire so sincere not receive and answer? Is the desire itself false? Underlying this is the struggle between the search for meaning and the fear of failure, between cynicism and the natural hopes and aspirations of the heart. There is another fear also spoken of indirectly here, which perhaps tells us why the apparently ardent calling of the subject found no answer: the fear to be natural in oneself, to be be who one really is, full of deep desires, searching, possibly eccentric and risking mockery by the world. It is the fear of not being strong enough, due to which '*I keep my love hidden, unless it should vanish away.*'

The song ends not with a solution but with a provocation of the original question:

Food and drink have lost all interest to me,
my home life repels me,
relaxation and sleep
have turned against me like worst enemies.
Tell me, why is this happening?

This provocation is perhaps the key to an answer. What is this but a state of depression in which internal contradictions are preventing one from moving ahead? The apparently ardent calling, decorated with tears, is in fact only lukewarm: only when one is brave enough to stand up and do something with it, to declare it real despite the risk of ridicule, and to integrate it fully as part of one's life, will one's personality begin to flow naturally. Until then, life itself will seem to repel you, turning against you in the form of depression. Singing this song can then be considered as an act of bringing one's doubts and contradictions into the open, and asking over and over again, 'why, why, why?' until the point that one's love will no longer remain concealed away but will embody itself in action.

My purpose is not to interpret the songs so that there is nothing left for the reader, but to demonstrate their therapeutic value and the layers of meaning that can be read into them. This value lies not in the negating of difficult feelings, but in knowing how to guide and use their force, how to transform them, and in the recognition that apparent pole opposites are not always antagonistic to each other but rather the expression of a deeper harmony yet to be discovered. In the words of Rabindranath Tagore, whose own songs have expressed the same:

'The most important lesson that man can learn from his life is not that there is pain in the world, but rather that it depends on him to turn it into good account, that it is possible for him to transmute it into joy.'[4]

And describing the Baul tradition, which also shares its

wisdom through song:

'A devotee must utilize the compulsive power of his own emotion in trying to find union with God. And in loving God, he must be free from any motive other than the act of loving."[5]

That is to say, meditation for self-realisation, although a mental training and discipline of self-control on one hand, on the other can use the force of human feelings to its benefit. Not only can it, but it must, because between the first awakening of the spiritual search and its ultimate realisation, there is a long journey upon which meantime we must know what to do with ourselves, and how to flow naturally and enjoy the process along the way.

I have begun with examples of somewhat melancholic songs as these are feelings that we often try to avoid, or consider as obstacles without realising that not only are they inevitable, but also necessary. In Prabhat Samgiita it can be seen that although the lyrics may begin in a melancholic mood, they tend to end with some kind of realisation resulting from the said mood, and thus finally they are songs of hope and positivity. The same process of expression and transmutation of feeling can be used in any other context. For example, song number 1530 addresses the feeling of romantic love and longing:

Tell me, beautiful-eyed one,
why your hurt feelings?

Who was that Mysterious Visitor who came,
loved you a moment, and then went away?

After capturing your heart and mind,
He left, only to smile teasingly from afar.

Song 3039 moves in the same flow:

Why do You stay so far away,
smiling, in Your maddening way?

In despair,
my braided hair has come undone,
the black liner around my eyes
has been washed away by tears.

Another common theme is that of shyness and hesitation, and the desire for familiarity:

My mind longs to gaze on Him forever,
but out of shyness and fear I hesitate to look. (Song 11)

Remove all my shame and fear
so that we can come close to one another
and I can express myself freely with an open-heart. (Song 969)

Shyness and fear then become the joy of unity:

Whatever fear and shyness I had,
every last drop was taken away.
I could not comprehend what then happened:
everything disappeared in oneness,
merged completely into an all-encompassing light.
(Song 2461)

This ecstatic union is, more often and not, combined with a sense of wonder and surprise as to how an experience so expansive, so much greater than what one had imagined possible, could be contained within an ordinary human being. Not a saint or any revered figure, but any one of us:

With a little clay lamp in hand
I had been waiting to one side,
when You appeared before me
with the brilliance of countless suns. (Song 84)

From where and why this gift came, no one knows:

Why this awakening? In answer to whose call?
Day and night, continuously, I am seeking to know Him
from whom this call has come.
The newly blossomed morning-light spreads out,
the dawn-bird flaps its freshly-opened wings,
and my Friend, my Eternal Friend,
is covered in golden light. (Song 6)

The possible ways in which human sentiments can be expressed, interpreted and transformed are multifarious and clearly extend beyond a simple conflict between 'repression' and 'expression'. The Freudian scheme of human life as a continuous state of discontent due to repression of baser instincts is,[6] in the context of mysticism, not only an erroneous one, but indeed a dreary and highly unimaginative view of human emotional life. Certainly human beings come with a strong set of impulses and egoistic desires, but it is the very friction caused by them which leads one to seek beyond them, almost as if they exist in order to surpass themselves. Freedom lies in discovering the way and means to utilise and propel the mind towards an ever-expanded sense of self, and day to day emotions are considered as metaphors of a deeper spiritual search, not the other way around. If anything, as a society we have the tendency to 'repress' our potential and depth of the human experience through a peculiar fear of 'repressing' the ego, which arises from not understanding its nature or how to mould it.

The mystical scheme of emotions is a liberating and creative one: in it day and night dance around each other seeking harmony; love seeks to expand itself from personal possession to include the entire creation and natural world; destitution leads to renewal; loneliness and separation are cultivated into a longing for union; and through all this we discover a natural flow of feeling and the true meaning of spontaneity which culminates in the all-pervasive joy of being. Most importantly, perhaps, is the realization that the paints and paintbrushes are in our own hands, the canvas in front of us, waiting for us to take the confidence to choose what to do with the colours of the mind. Again, in the words of the poet Sohrab Sepehri:

'Let us constantly create our own two borders,
and every minute liberate them.
Let us go, let us go, whispering of the absence of borders.'[7]

Through the friction of our limitations, seeking freedom and in love with the essence of life, let us surpass those very limitations, again and again until infinity.

MYSTICISM AND NATURE

A grand part of the symbolism in Prabhat Samgiita is taken directly from the natural world. Taken simply as they are, the descriptions of nature are beautiful and touch the heart, but to understand the inner meaning of the songs, their symbolic import needs to be grasped. They are expressions of experiences that are at once intangible, and yet very real. Some are also well established symbols, like that of the lotus flower representing the purity of mind maintained even amongst the trammels of life.

Take, for example, song, 911, which sings of Suvarna Rekha, the 'river of gold.' This is a real river in Bengal, but more importantly, it is the river of the mind, flowing towards the infinity of the ocean.

There is a path by the seashore,
leading across the dunes.
When the sun rises there,
the sky and the sea blossom with colour,
awakening an infinite joy within my mind.

Coloured birds dance amidst cashew-nut orchards,
as seagulls fly across to distant, unknown lands.

Releasing his boat,
the sailor sets out on his journey.
Pulled by the far-reaching song of the river's current,
he moves swiftly towards the sea…

The sun here is rising not only upon the dunes, but within the heart, which blossoms with the awakening of spiritual joy. The birds again are the mind, searching and crossing the limits of the self, the boat a human being setting out on the river of life.

A flower is never only a flower, it is a person whose heart, hidden beneath the petals, is preparing to bloom, revealing the sweet nectar and aroma within. A dewdrop is the apparent insignificance of human life, capable of reflecting the grandeur of the mountains within it. The vast sky is infinity; the sunrise hope and awakening; the dark night is sometimes despair waiting for the dawn, other times the intimacy of solitude, a moment for meeting with the self. Everything is not only what it first appears, but something more, perhaps many things.

In the first section of songs, there are included compositions about the various seasons. These are deeply metaphorical statements about the changing phases of the human mind and the necessity of each of them. It is especially worth mentioning the songs of rain and storm: the monsoon rains, arriving at the end of summer, although disruptive, are celebrated as a symbol of change, movement and revitalisation. Life, after all, depends on them. The storms, winds and rain should not be confused for negative symbols, or for torments of the mind.[18] Rain and storms are common themes of Indian music, and in their use as metaphors is contained a very astute observation of the human mind: static calm is not what makes us happy. It is dynamic movement, the stirring of the mind to new possibilities, the hope of change and renovation, that brings us delight. The thunder and lightening of the storm are not fearful. They are hopeful, and hope excites and gives meaning to life.

Ensconced in the metaphors of nature is the inner realisation of creation as an embodiment of the sacred, and the recognition that humanity will not come to know the infinite through separation from the world, but through the world itself. Song 1114 is an example of ecstasy through and in nature:

...the dust of the earth, dancing,
speaks of its constant desire for You;

the sweetly-blowing sandal breeze
is saying that there exists none but You;
the rugged ocean waves
forever look to You;
the glittering stars in the far-off sky,
shining, offer their worship;

the dewdrops are Your tears of delight,
the monsoon-rains are pouring Your love and affection;
the sweet smell of flowers
carries the message of Your infinitude...

Here the dust of the earth until the stars of the sky are at once longing for the divine and are divinity embodied. In this state, everything and everywhere one looks, divine longing and divinity is to be found, and thus surrounded on all sides, we transform into the same.

In this spirit, ecology and spirituality also

harmoniously intertwine. Spirituality helps develop a sense of wonder and union with nature, and creates and ecological awareness based not only on the scientific observation of the interconnectedness and interdependence of life on earth, but on a lived experience of the same. We need the natural world not only because without her we cannot survive physically, but because she has an existential value in and of herself. Without her we cannot survive emotionally or spiritually, because life would lose the subtle delight of a beauty created by an artist whom we do not know but seek, consciously or unconsciously, to understand.

MYSTICISM AND SOCIETY

The last section of songs are placed under the title of 'social and environmental conscience,' as a recognition of the fact, as was the vision of P. R. Sarkar himself, that the internal expansion produced by meditative practices should, and indeed must if it is to have any lasting value, facilitate a parallel expansion of social conscience. This is best expressed in his philosophy of 'neo-humanism', explained as humanism expanded to include the entire created world, and resting upon the perennial inspiration of a universal spirituality.[19]

They are mostly songs designed to inspire one to empathise with the collective pain and hope of humanity and the earth as a living entity, to do something positive for the world despite the obstacles, and to promote the concept of a united human society based not on homogeneity but on diversity. Song 1892, for example, reminds us of the capacity of each individual to facilitate change, and challenges the presumption that power always lies in hands other than our own:

Oh dust particle,
oh speck of dust,
you are tiny, yet you are great.

The whole history of the world lies hidden within you.
Spread out your wings, oh messenger of the new era!

Our power as human beings lies as much as anything, the song tells us, like the beauty of life, in simple things, in our daily interactions, in our authenticity as people, just as the earth's beauty is formed from many particles of dust:

Who says you have no beauty to offer?
Who says you have no flame to kindle the incense?
It is you who, as the red-ocre earth,
beautifies the green fields,
the moist scent of which makes our minds turn dreamy and contemplative.

The section ends with a subtly symbolic song reminding us that even as we enter into a new era (the tender red leaves sprouting), we must remember and respect both the accomplishments and mistakes of history (the fallen yellow leaves). Who we are and what we will become depends on the wisdom and lessons we are able to take from our collective past:

Tender red leaves sprout on the tree branches.
Old leaves blown are away by spring storms.

The faded yellow leaves, dried and colourless,
have fallen, neglected and lifeless like the dust.

Don't forget the fallen leaves.
Their stories should also be written:
through their history of light and shadow,
darkness can be removed. (5004)

The same can said of the collective as of an individual's internal world: light and shadow both exist, and must. What is important is the understanding that we glean from them and the future that this comprehension will impart. The passing truths of life are whispering and dancing back and forwards with deeper, intangible ones, and this dance shall go on, forever without end.

SEASONS AND NATURE

1114

The starry sky tells me
that there is one, only one, true Friend;*
the dust of the earth, dancing,
speaks of its constant desire for You;

the sweetly-blowing sandal breeze
is saying that there exists none but You;
the rugged ocean waves
forever look to You;
the glittering stars in the far-off sky,
shining, offer their worship;

the dewdrops are Your tears of delight,
the monsoon-rains are pouring Your love and affection;
the sweet smell of flowers
carries the message of Your infinitude;
every cell of the mind sings endlessly,
life after life,
of You, the Timeless Visitor.

Bandhu, the Eternal Friend who remains with you forever and always.

94

You came with the trembling cold of winter.
Who are You?
And what kind of beauty is this?

Covering the green earth with snow,
who are You?
What kind of beauty is this?

In the icy cold of the northern winds,
upon the leafless trees by the roadside,
You have written a cryptic message.
What wretchedness is this, what miserliness?

Life shivers in the icy storm,
the creepers and plants, vitality lost,
sing a strange song.
Why this hard-heartedness intermingled with your love?
What kind of beauty is this?

91

In the frosty air at the end of autumn,
why doesn't the lotus flower bloom?

Why don't the bees hover around the nectar-less flowers?
Though in the forest the lotus* does not bloom,
it is blooming inside my mind;
though around the flowers the bees don't gather,
they gather around the pollen of my heart.

The forest is filled with a sad song,
the melancholic tune of autumn,
and yet, thinking of Him,
pain and sadness disappear.

Although the flowers
have been robbed of their sweet fragrance,
fragrance will keep flowing through our songs,
and with that blessing we shall create a new world.

*Blooming of the lotus: the spiritual unfolding of the self.

104

With a rhythmic dance,
spring comes.
With a dancing beat, she comes.

The mist covered trees, smiling, sparkle with light,
fresh flowers and budding leaves adorn the earth,
like unbound hair let loose to dance across the open sky,
to the excited rhythm of the purvash* dance:
nature is decorated with the sweet beauty of spring.

Sea-breeze waves surge forth,
laughing upon the warm ocean water,
as tides of mellifluous delight come and go,
the mind flowing unbroken
in thoughts of He who is the source of this sweet
splendour.

*An oriental dance with quick, fleeting movements.

3110

Spring buds hint at the arrival of new life,
as the Un-Aging One plays hide-and-seek
among the songs of spring.

The wild-flowers laugh,
fragrance drifts upon the breeze,
and the sky is filled with the cuckoo's song,
pulsating with vitality.

Fresh sweetness flows upon the earth,
eyes, looking upwards, are filled with new light,
and resonating with presence of the Ever-Fresh One,*
a great love tugs at the depths of the heart.

Infinite consciousness, beyond the bounds of time and decay, expressed through the youthful delight and freshness of spring.

1682

Spring has arrived,
and the earth is dressed up joyfully.
The living-world abounds
with colours, forms and movement.
Oh artist of creation, come before me,
rest Your open eyes and sweet smile upon me.
Come, pause a while,
Your enchantment revealed upon the earth.

Oh King of kings,
only You know the meaning of Your mysterious game!*
All is filled with love, and yet,
you bring tears to my eyes.
Oh gallant, Unashamed One,
With rhythmic dancing, enter inside my timid heart.

---

* Liila: the divine and incomprehensible game or drama of creation.

1170

Who was that Unexpected Traveller*
that I met in the palash forest?**

Who was that Timeless Traveller
who whispered lovingly in my ears?

Springs comes,
filled with the fiery red of palash flowers.
The whole forest awakens,
vibrating with the passion and rhythm of life.

Who is this Mysterious Traveller,
so near and yet so far?
Intellect and logic
cannot comprehend Him.

Who is this Unexpected Visitor?

---

*A personification of the inner awakening of consciousness within an individual.
**Palash: flame of the forest trees, which in spring in Bengal are covered in brilliant red flowers before the leaves appear.

1540

With dry-leaves as its dancer's ankle-bells
the storm enters,
with its terrible song and dance of destruction.

Accompanied by the rhythmic movement
of tal palms and tamal trees
and the perfume of tuberoses at night,
the impact of the huge storm encroaches,
under the stern gaze of the god of death.

Beyond the bounds of praise and condemnation,
as it moves in an intoxicated frenzy,
from a gap between the battling of the dark clouds,
a beam of light emerges.

112

Destructive clouds have gathered,
fierce winds blow,
the summer storms of Kalboishakhi* have come,
the ruinous summer storms have come.

Closing their windows and doors to the thunder and wind,
everyone sits inside
listening to the storm-dance of the rain.

So many precious trees have been uprooted,
the fruits have all fallen in the storm,
the birds lament,
having lost their nests to the hail and the wind.

In the summer heat the god of terror and tempests
in thunderous form dances wildly,
as the ships in the water, full of dread,
toss and sway upon the waves.

Destructive summer thunderstorms that take place a few times every year during of slightly before the Bengali month of Baishakh (early April) in Bangladesh and West Bengal.

3663

Rain arrives,
carrying the promise of a green and verdant earth,
and upon that hope is carried your love-filled song.

The waterfowl call-out once again,
the swallows no longer search for water,
and like the flow of creation, the peacock's tail dances;
upon the rain's rhythmic tune, the pandan* flowers bloom,
their sweet scent stirring the heart.

On the banks of the lake, frogs croak,
bumble-bees thrust themselves
into the pollen of the kadamb** flowers,
and beyond the mist, on the other side of the shore,
within the inner-mind, unseen, a guiding star shines.

---

*Screw-pine, an aromatic plant with flowers which are distilled to make a scented water, somewhat like rose-water.
**A round, pom-pom like flower with a yellow centre covered with small white blossoms, that blooms during the rainy season.

3720

These gloomy monsoon rains!
My mind drifts upon the clouds,
floating amidst the deep green
of the graceful bamboo forest.

Beloved, won't You come, playing Your flute,
stirring the depths of the river's* calm waters,
the viina's** emotive melody taking hold of my mind?
I ask myself, is this really true love?

As the sound of rain pours down outside,
breaking the earth's inertia,
inside, seen by no one, tears flood my eyes.
As the world is lost in this tearful flow of rain,
I wonder, will You return again?

*The Yamuna river, also a symbol of the inner flow leading to self-realisation.
**The Indian lute or lyre, a string-instrument.

5011

Clouds, clouds, so many clouds,
today the sky is full of clouds!

I sit at home with nothing to do…

The rice seedlings are drying up,
the lemon flowers fall from the trees,
the custard apples' blossoms blacken,
the farmers' heads ring in the heat.

The earth will become fresh and green again,
ponds filled with water.
The boatmen will start their work again,
boats loaded with produce.

911

Oh my Dearest Friend,*
come to my village,
on the banks of the Suvarna Rekha** river,
come to the banks of this very river.

There is a path by the seashore,
leading across the dunes.
When the sun rises there,
the sky and the sea blossom with colour,
awakening an infinite joy within my mind.

Coloured birds dance amidst cashew-nut orchards,
as seagulls fly across to distant, unknown lands.

Releasing his boat,
the sailor sets out on his journey.
Pulled by the far-reaching song of the river´s current,
he moves swiftly towards the sea,
leaving all his worries behind.

Bandhu: the Eternal Friend who remains with you forever and always.
**A river in Bengal, literally 'the river of gold.'*

1908

Dewdrop,
oh tiny dewdrop,
the whole world is reflected within you,
the whole ocean realised.

The great lies within the small,
Your beauty hidden within every atom and molecule.
You are accessible to all.

You are embodied within the silver of starry galaxies,
in the natural world,
in the results of meditation,
in all the diverse rhythms and varied expressions of life.

SADNESS, SOLITUDE AND MELANCHOLY

122

You came alone, oh Traveller,
at dawn when the night-jasmine* had already fallen.
Seeing my door closed,
You stood waiting by the roadside.

My eyes still cloaked with sleep,
I could not see clearly.
Evaporating like the wet dew of dawn,
You departed.

The jasmine vine at my door
still resonates with your message.
As the dew-drops disappear,
I am left with only the hope of Your return.

If my door had been open when You came,
we could have spoken,
I could have merged that autumn night
Into Your divine, melodious flow.

Shuili, a small aromatic flower with white petals and a saffron centre which blooms at night and falls to the ground at dawn.

656

Who is singing in this broken heart of mine?
Who is singing this song today?

The vibration of an unknown melody
fills the sky and air,
and without any inhibitions,
stirs the inaccessible depths of my heart.

All disappointments disappear
as a flow of ambrosial melodies,
beautiful effulgence,
and a sweet flood of affection
envelop the earth.
Who is it that moves the heavens to this mysterious tune?

Who is it singing today,
In this broken heart of mine?

792

If You love me, come,
come to me...

If you start weighing all my faults and virtues,
You won't find even a trace of goodness:
my garden is full of thorns,
there aren't any blossoming flowers.
There are, however, many unopened flower buds,
which, if You would come and sit inside them,
would open up and bloom.

I haven't any real love or devotion,
the pollen of my heart drifts not upon the breeze,
but Your touch would vibrate
the hidden depths of my heart
with intoxicating fragrance and joyful laughter.

461

Tell me,
for whom do you sit waiting,
upon this lonely river bank?

As I row the boat of form
upon the formless ocean,
no one is ever forgotten.

My boat flows upon the eternal stream of time,
whose beginning and end
neither philosophy nor science can understand.
I flow ever ahead without pause.

At the end of a tiring day,
as all return to their own homes,
a weary traveller approaches the river's bank
in need of a boat:
I am always waiting with my boat,
I never delay, I am never late.

4455

Who are You, oh Unknown One?
Arriving all of a sudden, You broke my slumber,
I know not why.

Asleep in a deep and dreadful darkness,
with all the windows bound fast shut,
I did not come to the door to receive You,
and yet, in spite of that, You appeared before me:
opening my eyes,
I was bathed in a flood of compassion and light.

I have no idea where I was or how I'd come there:
recounting stories of my past,
You told me: 'don't cry-
all these door and windows, slumber and awakening,
are just acts of My imagination.'

2182

Why are you sitting around?
What work have you finished?
Can you give me the balance-sheet of your work done?

After all the buying and selling,
what actually remains left over?

Between sunrise and sunset
you inhaled and exhaled so many times,
and now, in the evening of life,
can you tell me, what work you have actually done?

At the dawn of life you passed time playing and reading,
then you were busy in money-making,
and now you are sitting around counting stars.
Tell me, what is to be made of this?

4185

Morning to evening, I sit in solitude, thinking:
'There is no one in all the three worlds I can call my own.
I am alone, completely alone.'

I watch the sun rise and set,
the moon as it arrives, smiling,
but they do not stop for me.
I am alone, completely and utterly alone.

Who is it that moves the sun?
Who is it that gives the evening moon its smile?
Only that essence will remain eternally.
I desire Him alone,
for Him I sing with all my heart.

809

Which new vibration,
which melody,
is it that strums today, upon the lute of my heart?

Upon which faith,
upon which hope,
did You call me to leave my house
amidst the pouring monsoon rains?

The roses had shed all their petals,
left only with their thorns,
their pollen robbed of its sweet fragrance.
Into this dried-up, flow-less river,
how is it that You came,
summoning an up-surging flood
in the river* of my mind?

The light of festivity had gone from my life,
a blanket-cover of gloom had descended upon me.
Into this life robbed of meaning,
how is it that You came,
flooding the empty void of my heart
with freshly-dawning light?

*The Yamuna river, also symbolic of an inner flow leading to self-realisation.

3039

If You love me,
why don't You come closer to me?
Why do You stay so far away,
smiling, in Your maddening way?

In despair,
my braided hair has come undone,
the black liner around my eyes
has been washed away by tears.

Everything is part of Your beautiful creation:
I heard that all exist within Your mind,
so full of sweetness,
like garden arches covered with climbing flowers.

81

Under a dream-like spell,
the days pass on by,
never to return,
as is the unchangeable way of things.

Words once spoken, suffering endured,
all dissolve into infinity.

Whatever began in the distant past,
the first beginnings are yet more ancient still.
On a thread of dreams,
in the depths of the heart, the viina* weaves its melodies.
Those who depart, forever lost to us,
go on to merge into Your infinite vibrational flow.

Indian lute of lyre, a stringed instrument.

<u>3320</u>

I called out to You,
I called and called,
why didn't You listen?
My eyes were filled with tears.
Why didn't You respond?

The world deliberately deceives me,
will You also do the same?
Filled with fear, I keep my love hidden
unless it should vanish away.

Why didn't You listen to my ardent calling?

Food and drink have lost all interest to me,
My home life repels me,
Relaxation and sleep
have turned against me like worst enemies,
Tell me, why is this happening?

Why didn't You respond to my tearful calls?

2142

Evening star, Oh evening star,
why do you stay awake, alone in the distant sky?
Upon whose path do you gaze?
About whom are you thinking?

"Tell me," said the star,
"who has refused to speak to you?
Tears of sadness run in your eyes.
Get up and dance with the rhythm of life!

I feel your pain,
and sing to that same tune,
moving in that same rhythm.
Don't you know who I am, awake in the sky?"

823

Sitting waiting for You,
I thread a garland of fresh flower petals,
pouring into it the sweetness of my heart.

At night's end,
the night-jasmine* flowers,
carrying dewdrops of pain,
fall to the ground.
In their sorrowful tears
I can see my own story.

In the hearts of those who thread their garlands
with sincerity and dedication,
a flame blazes.
Do You know how much I must endure
because of this flame that burns inside my heart?

Shiuli, a small aromatic flower with white petals and a saffron centre which blooms at night and falls to the ground at dawn.

LOVE AND LONGING

1570

Who are you thinking of all the time,
beautiful-eyed one,
as you stare out at the road?
Who is that Captivating One,
That has stolen away your heart?

You desired nothing
except to offer your own self,
and you got what you wanted:
your heart has been taken away somewhere….

Today, you sing the story
of your heartfelt love and longing,
your heart filled with deep feeling,
your eyes with flowing tears.

1530

Tell me,
oh beautiful, doe-eyed one,
why your wounded feelings?
Tell me why.

Tell me,
why is there no song upon your red lips?

Why is there no white scented jasmine in your black hair,
no earrings dangling from your ears?
Why haven't you decorated your braids with the irresistible
beauty of flowers?
What happened to the shine of your moon-like face?

Tell me, beautiful-eyed one,
why your hurt feelings?

Who was that Mysterious Visitor* who came,
loved you a moment, and left?
After capturing your heart and mind,
He left, smilingly teasing you from afar.

Tell me, beautiful-eyed one
why your wounded pride?

A personification of the inner awakening of consciousness within an individual.

2049

Sitting alone by the window,
I think only of Him:
who was that visitor, from an unknown land,
overflowing with love,
filling my pain with sweetness?

In my free time, alone,
I see His love in the crimson red of dawn.
In work too, I am always thinking of Him.

Even if I forget Him,
He does not forget me.
The musical tinkling of His viina*
reminds me of His enchanting face,
as my life moves with His infinite flow.

---

*The Indian lute or Lyre, a stringed instrument.

12

His eyes filled with affection
and a smile like the shine of pearls,
the Unknown Traveller* has arrived!

My tender heart beats quickly:
what is this irresistible feeling that overwhelms me?
Who is it this Unknown Traveller creating such a flow of
bliss within?

My mind longs to gaze upon Him forever,
but out of shyness and fear I hesitate to look.
I wonder, where was this sweetness hidden until now?

A personification of the inner awakening of consciousness within an individual.

1027

I seek You alone, oh Infinite One!
Although You surround me on all sides,
I have exhausted myself searching and searching.

You exist at once within the tumultuous ocean waves
and in the sweet cooing of birds amidst forest-solitude;
You are there silent and ever-present
upon all the roads I walk,
oh Infinite One!

In the sky when clear-blue,
and also when scattered with stars;
in gardens and forests,
and in the sweet essence of flowers,
You are the eternal peace
existing within all that is comprehensible
and also that which is beyond comprehension.

152

In sweet dreams among fragrant magnolia trees,
in the magical mirror of my mind, I saw Him.

An enchanting fragrance upon the gentle breeze,
with wonder-filled eyes,
I saw Him there, at the river's banks.

Flower-pollen drifting in and out from an unknown land,
the peacock of my inner-mind
gazes longingly towards the blue sky,
opening its fan-like tail.

On lonely, late-night, moonlit paths,
my heart, overflowing with love,
dances and dances around Him.

4729

Listen, listen, listen,
my Eternal Friend,* so far away,
listen to me.

It seems You know me well,
so why don't You reveal Yourself?

In the crimson dawn we met each other,
and this memory stays with me day and night.
You are always watching over me,
this truth I know.

So close and yet so far,
around and around You I move,
smiling and crying I sing.
Pull me closer, closer still.

Bandhu: the Eternal Friend who remains with you forever and always.

3570

Through life and death,
light and darkness,
You are my only acquaintance:

Oh formless, Beloved One,
infinite consciousness beyond the bounds of thought,
You entered within the ocean of forms
and offered me Your love:
I am but a tiny bubble of foam
upon the vast ocean of Your body-
I know none but You.

Upon the surging tides, in quest of You, I came,
smiling and dancing
under the pull of Your moonlit-waves:
every movement, every ebb and flow,
occurs within this captivating dream of Yours.
Within that dream are the weavings
of so many imaginary, enchanting colours.

1187

Created from Your love,
and resonant with Your music,
memory of that experience
remains fresh even until this day,
stirring the inner depths of my being.

Recollection of that smile transports my mind:
the sound of that flute, that flow of notes,
mesmerises me completely,
immersing me in divine love.
On hearing that irresistible call,
my limited identity is completely swept away!

That blissful-joy makes my mind dance;
That stream of melody causes me to transcend myself;
and that brilliant radiance awakens my consciousness,
flooding everything with light.

4022

Oh King of my mind,
I love You!
Like the night-jasmine flowers* bathed in dew,
I fall on the path at Your feet.

All the stories of the evening sky,
all the pain of the thick midnight darkness,
all tales of the last hours of night,
at dawn are offered to You.

The chirping of birds as the crimson sun rises,
the noon-time garlanded in bright rays of sun,
and the dappled colours of candle-light in the evening,
all decorate my tray of offerings,
prepared ready to welcome You with love.

*Shiuli, a small aromatic flower with white petals and a saffron centre which blooms at night and falls to the ground at dawn.

2036

The crescent moon in the sky
alone is enough to light up the earth.
You are the full-moon: reveal your complete form,
and fill the expanse of my inner-consciousness
with Your light.

You are the boundless ocean of consciousness,
illuminating every living cell.
Clouds may come and go
but You are impossible to forget.

Consciously or unconsciously,
all long for You,
and are bought closer to You by the bonds of love.
You exist, and therefore I exist,
in this divinely-sweet flow of Yours.

148

Waves of light move upon light:
the world is filled with light,
everything is immersed in an ocean of light,
and my heart overflows with light.

Although I am just like a tiny candle flame,
and although I have a red bindu* on my forehead,
I have only ever loved You,
I have loved only You,
my soul has lost itself in You.

That this tiny flame
has loved and lost itself in You,
this is the culmination of all knowledge,
there is nothing more left to understand.

I understand only this,
I know just this much:
that this little light has been lost in your light,
and I have been filled with Your with your ever-present being.

You filled me,
You came and filled me with Your being,
and this little flame was completely absorbed into You.

*Bindu, a red dot placed between the eyes, commonly used after marriage .

696

You are like a hundred-petalled golden lotus,*
so beautiful that I hesitate to draw near.
Because of Your spiny foliage,
I fear to approach You.

Remove all of my shame and fear
so that we can come close to one another
and I can express myself freely with an open-heart.
I don't want to remain far away any more.

Your sweet nectar** is sought after by everyone,
and it is for a taste of that honey
that I stay up awake, waiting...
Your grandeur, Your intoxicating fragrance,
cannot be expressed with words.

---

*Symbol of the sahasrara cakra, the seat of pure consciousness within the human body, at the crown of the head.
**The blissful substance/sensation released (from the sahasrara cakra) upon experiencing spiritual union.

2046

Come to my home:
with tearful eyes, I have waited so long to welcome You.

You know everything about me,
there are no secrets, no formalities, between us.
My mind, moving towards You,
spreads out its wings into the endless sky.

I love you as my very own,
without shyness or fear.
Your form is boundless, your qualities unlimited:
this is what I have come to understand.

2725

The river's song flows on,
brushing aside anything in its way,
focused totally towards the ocean,*
the objective of it's Dhyána.**

The boat,*** in sweet motion, moves on
past the stories and songs on the river's****banks.
Rushing towards Him single-mindedly,
in that flow of thought, pain and suffering are forgotten.

The river of my mind desires You alone,
bind it not to mundane thoughts:
humbly, I solicit You,
break down all rocky-obstructions along the river's way.

*Ocean: infinite consciousness.
**Dhyána: meditation practice in which the mind moves in a ceaseless flow towards its goal.
***Boat: human being.
****River: life.

2657

Where the sky touches the sea,
upon that line of light,
at that horizon-line of the sky,
I search for You.

I know that the blue sky has no end,
that it never actually touches the ocean,
yet foolishly, I keep on thinking this way.

You are the invisible dance of beauty
within the innermost core of the heart.
Moving around and around You,
the strings of the heart vibrate in joy.

579

Don't go away,
don't leave!
Don't You love those who love You so much?

As the moonlight glances furtively at the flowers blooming
on the balcony,
my mind bathes in the colours
of the moonlit-painted night.

Once mysterious and unknown,
You are now familiar me.
Don't you understand this feeling of mine,
don't You understand?

Dear to all,
You fill every heart with sweet tenderness.
Between pain, humiliation and joy
You remain the unwavering Friend* of all.
Don't forget this fact, don't forget it.

*Bandhu: the Eternal Friend who remains with you forever and always.

2431

A bee came and stole away all the pollen
from inside the flower bud.

Who was that mysterious bee,
smiling,
capturing the heart in just the blink of a moment?

The petals where He neglects to land accumulate dirt,
weeping, they wither and fall,
not understanding what has befallen them.

The honey-filled flowers
with all their heart and mind sing:
come, oh Bee, come, oh Incomparable One,
make the climbing creeper of hope reach upwards!

ECSTASY AND AWAKENING

6

My Friend, my eternal Friend,*
is enveloped in golden light.

Anointed with the sweet pollen of the heart,
the bird of dawn-awakening is roused to sing.

Why this awakening? In answer to whose call?
Day and night, continuously,
I am seeking to know Him
from whom this call has come.
The newly blossomed morning-light spreads out,
the dawn-bird flaps its freshly-opened wings,
and my Friend, my eternal Friend,
is covered in golden light.

**Bandhu: the Eternal Friend who remains with you forever and always.*

130

The golden dawn of my life, is it returning again?
Piercing the darkness of countless pains,
countless agonies, countless humiliations.

How many twilights, how many dawns,
how many autumn and spring nights,
how many hopes and aspirations
have all passed by, floating away in tears?

On the eastern horizon the crimson dawn smiles.
The fragrance of flowers floats in the air.
With the new delight of the new year,
all painful memories vanish away.

84

With a little clay lamp in hand
I had been waiting to one side,
when You appeared before me
with the brilliance of countless suns.

Wave upon wave broke out upon the surging ocean,
like a frenzied battle-cry bursting forth
from the frothy, foaming stream of life.

Innumerable atoms and molecules rushed forth
in a wildly-restless song.
Rushing from here to there
in a storm of electrically-charged lightening, they moved,

when You appeared before me,
as I stood waiting to one side,
my little clay lamp in hand.

1199

Jingling, jingling,
to the tinkling sound of a dancer's ankle bells,
come, come, oh Incomparable One!

Into the expansive freedom of the open sky
all my mistakes dissolve,
they dissolve away…

The southern breeze, the dancing peacock of my mind,
towards what do they run?
They run after You, longing for You,
Oh Beloved One.

Today, the chariot of light moves on ahead.
The stream, shivering with delight, murmurs softly.
Illuminated by Your touch,
they offer their salutations to You.

1774

You are mingled in the flow of tears,
in the smiling flowers,
oh Compassionate One,
pouring love,
the essence of sweetness.

Today by Your grace I understood
that You are truly mine.
Come into the depths of my heart!
Nobody will know, so why hesitate?

How many lives have passed,
how many deaths, to bring this sweetness?
My movement around You
today has borne meaning,
in this beautiful flow.

709

Who has come?
Who has entered into the inaccessible depths of my heart?
Who has awakened within my life, within my world?

The door out of the dark prison cell opened,
the static gloom broken,
the sound of the anahata* ringing out in fresh song.

Calculations of what has been given and taken
become meaningless,
looking back to the past seems pointless,
when both the world and the depths of the heart
are pervaded with Your presence.

*Anahata cakra, located near the heart.

2651

In this ever-moving world,
those who came also departed.
Their footsteps remain on the dust
and in the midst of our minds.

Nothing upon this earth happens in vain:
not the joyful smiles, nor the tears of pain.
Both flow on together in the river of life,
as it passes sometimes through the desert,
and other times adorned with nature's beauty.

Those who have departed are present in Your soul,
and dance around You with their minds set free.
You are the shelter of the world,
embodiment of pure consciousness,
beyond the limits of perception.
Your sweetness rings in the hearts of all.

13

Having laughed, danced and sung,
enamoured with the moonlight,
I then placed protected
in the inner treasure-chest of my heart
all that I had seen, heard or experienced.

Lost and defeated by the raging of merciless storms,
I took the protection of Him in whom all is finally lost.

Realising that a place without light is a lifeless place,
I searched for and today attained the God of divine light.

2461

My eyes, acknowledging no restrictions,
long to gaze upon Your benevolent form.
Whether in mountains, caves, or anywhere in the world,
I always keep You guarded within the innermost,
inaccessible regions of my heart.

In the daylight and also in the dark of night,
within all the good and evil of the world,
in this play of light and shadow,
this enchanting divine game,
Your flow of sweetness is intermingled.

Whatever fear and shyness I had,
every last drop was taken away.
I could not comprehend what then happened:
everything disappeared in oneness,
merged completely in an all-encompassing light.

57

My individual rhythm moves together with the pulsating
beat of a timeless dance:
in a flow of ideation my feelings of duality melt away.

Whatever I have thought, whatever I have done,
my wishes were for all.
From door to door, house to house,
from one heart to another, I went,
sharing the sweet scent of magnolia flowers blooming.

My own rhythm shall inspire all to dance,
my own struggles shall give life to all.
Transported to a far away realm
by the tune of an enchanting song, I returned,
bringing a flow of divine sweetness along with me.

3147

A lotus* of joy bloomed upon the lake,
its fragrance drifting upon the dawn breeze.

Impossible to see externally, it exists within the mind.
Within the heart it bloomed, something rare in all the three
worlds.**

Glowing with purity, eyes towards the sun,
ever-awake and filled with the sun's light,
although attached to its stem in the water,
it touches not the slime,
smiling in delight, thrilled by the ever-lively manifestations
of Your divine game,***

Let this lake of my mind my never dry up,
fed by the snow,
remaining full throughout the summer heat,
vibrant with the motion of waves of love,
age after age, shall it remain pure, clear and beautiful.

---

*The spiritual unfolding of the mind, and a symbol of mental purity.
**The entire creation, past, present and future.
***Liila, the divine and incomprehensible game of creation.

2487

Rhythmically,
with dancing beats, You came.
Where You then went, I don't know.

I cannot comprehend why this awakening happened,
upon the shoreline of the lake of my mind,
beyond the periphery of words.

The Charioteer of Light,
You come and go as you please, at no fixed time,
Your unlimited offering of affection
expressed through this divine game of creation.

You love all, and all love You:
Your store of grace
is unequalled in all the seven worlds. *
You exist, therefore I exist,
nourished by Your flow of compassion.
By remaining ever with You,
my spiritual pursuit attains its fulfilment.

Lokas, or layers of existence within creation, from the crude material world to the subtle spiritual realms.

3020

On the barren desert path, a spring of sweet water,
at the end of hot and troubled day, a cooling balm:
Your sweetness is mingled everywhere.

Age after age, I longed for You,
the cessation of desire,
and the fulfilment of our deepest desires.
Today You came, indescribably beautiful.

Ecstasy breaks all bonds,
such that I am unable to think or act.
Formlessness has taken form
upon the dust of the earth itself.

1303

What is this impatient sweetness,
this overflowing stream of light?

With what ecstatic joy does the river rush,
its silver touch washing darkness away?

What is this irrepressible wave of consciousness,
this intoxicating mellifluence,
like the calm silence of a deer
moving through the forest of the mind?

903

You came when the moon was full,
as it played hide and seek with the shifting clouds.

Amidst the galaxies painted in the far off sky
a young swan had lost its way.

So many moonlit nights came and went
but my heart remained empty.

Hearing the sound of Your approaching footsteps
my heart filled with joy.
That same swan found its path again.

335

To which unknown land do you go, my friend,
to which unknown land,
moving upstream* against the current,
carrying with you the sail-boat of the mind?

The boat un-moored from the river's bank
rushes ahead with the delirious speed of the storm.
Tell me, which melody has enchanted your mind?

The stormy night came,
blowing out the candle's light.
To which melody did you awake,
beside yourself with its song,
carried far away?

To which unknown land are you headed,
my friend,
in the sail-boat of the mind?

The upward flow of energy, of internal spiritual force, moving from crude to subtle, limited to unlimited.

STRUGGLE

<u>4370</u>

Rowing the boat of Your name,
I will cross the sea!

Caring not for the trials of fog, storms, or changing tides,
I am going to set out now and cross the vast ocean!

Whosoever may call me from behind,
whosoever may try to discourage me,
whatever threatening and frightful stories they may tell,
I will not listen, nor be deterred from my journey.

Yonder, across the violent and tempestuous waves,
lies a radiant, wave-less tranquillity:
beyond all transitory disturbances,
the call of eternal peace.

1070

Tell me,
who are you, standing on the path in my way?

You told me, 'leave that path,
I won't let you go the wrong way.'

There was a deep hole in front of me,
hidden by a curtain of darkness.
Unaware of it,
I would have fallen in.

I was imprisoned by arrogance:
You removed my pride of intellect, fame and renown,
and taught me the method of sa'dhana.*

The system of meditation designed with the aim of unifying the individual mind with infinite consciousness.

<u>3225</u>

As soon as I think I have understood something,
I realise that I really don't know anything,
I don't know anything…

Inexperienced, I was looking for a path
not knowing for what I searched.

Who was that Unexpected Visitor?*
In which mysterious stream am I being carried, further and further?
Seeking the unknown, I wander day and night,
confused, not knowing why.

Oh Compassionate One, what game** is this?
You always play with me, this insignificant person, in strange new ways.
Tell, me how long will this game between the individual and the divine go on?

*A personification of the inner awakening of consciousness within an individual.
**Liila: the divine and incomprehensible game or drama of creation.

1878

The clouds came and whispered in my ears:
'If storms come, don't you worry.
Don't you know
that both clouds and storms have the same origin?'

'The deep, contemplative ocean
and the restless, stormy waves
exist one within the other.
Don't forget this truth.'

'In one hand He holds a terrifying sword,
in the other an ambrosial fountain.
From His hands he gives blessings and fearlessness,*
His feet, liberation.
Remember this assurance of His.'

---

*Referring to the varabhaya mudra, a special gesture of blessing from Guru to disciple.

1036

You came, bringing light,
and driving away the darkness.

Smiling, You told me:
"When affected by fear,
open your eyes and think of me.
Thorn-less roses, high-tides without low-tides,
this is not the way of things.
You should understand this point.

I am with You and love You at all times,
throughout both joy and sorrow,
I am yours and you are mine,
so cast aside your misery and distress."

2540

I am aware that I have no virtues,
yet nonetheless, I am Yours.
Moving in Your flow,
this little heart of mine is full.

Whether I am sinful or sinless,
I do not know.
I only know that I must not leave Your path.
Through comings and goings, smiles and tears,
I remember you.

I know that You remain with me,
individually and as part of the collective.*
Please keep me moving under the shelter
of Your causeless grace.

*Ota Yoga and Prota Yoga: the intimate relationship of the infinite with an individual, and the general relation to creation, both of which exist simultaneously.

2789

The boat I released today,
let it move ahead unobstructed.
Unobstructed does not mean without obstacles,
but facing all obstacles, it should move on.

You are the fear-instilling fire of destruction,
the burnt skull carrying a message of annihilation.
You move within forms
both frightening and sweetly delightful,

in ever new forms, in every season,
sometimes pleasing, other times displeased:
show Your displeasure, but not Your indifference!
Don't withdraw Your flow of compassion!

SOCIAL AND ENVIRONMENTAL CONSCIENCE

647

Today You have come
to think about those who are suffering and in pain,
to remove darkness from every mind,
to love all living beings.

The earth had been waiting hopefully for your arrival,
her body covered with scars of distress,
all happiness faded until the point of disappearing
under a flow of unbearable sorrow.

Kindle a light on the bosom of mother earth!
Shining brighter and brighter,
generously pour sweet nectar into the centre of oppressed,
tender hearts
and send out a clear and unmistakable call
for all to move ahead with heads held high.

11

The red earth
dances on ahead of me.
You know, this earth is not merely soil,
she is my very own mother.

The fields full of paddy
gleam under the golden sunlight.
The people born of this soil
are genuine and righteous like pure gold.

Oh earth, my own Mother Earth!

With her starry sky, fragrant flowers,
sweet water and fresh air,
my Mother Earth with all of this,
consoles and calms my eyes.

Oh earth, my own Mother Earth!

My dearest, Eternal Friend,
if you really love me,
come close to me,
and with Your blessing
from this very day on,
I will help create a truthful and genuine humanity upon this earth.

Oh earth, my Mother Earth!

<u>1892</u>

Oh dust particle,
oh speck of dust,
you are tiny, yet you are great.

The whole history of the world lies hidden within you.
Spread out your wings, oh messenger of the new era!

Who says you have no life-force?
Who says you have no song?
There is life at every level, in every atom and molecule,
every particle is filled with song.

Who says you have no beauty to offer?
Who says you have no flame to kindle the incense?
It is you who, as the red-ochre earth,
beautifies the green fields,
the moist scent of which
makes our minds turn dreamy and contemplative.

1278

Some merge themselves in light,
others loose themselves in darkness;
some long for You alone,
others desire gifts and rewards;

some seek and rush towards Your effulgent light,
others, carrying out-dated skeletons of the past,
weep among the ruined bamboo groves;
some acknowledge and seek only Your hidden essence,
whilst others burn a flickering candle-flame
of divisive arguments
upon the name of Your divine and compassionate light.

Some, dancing in Your all-pervasive presence,
contented, desire nothing more.

1611

From the land of light, the smiling youth said:
'I will not be tricked by lies,
I will not cheat, nor will I be cheated!'

I will not be trapped
by the glitter of false promises,
no longer will I listen!

All are born seeking light,
but due to their greed and internal defects,
become entrapped in darkness,
tangled in self-constructed webs.

All human beings are part of one family,
sharing the same pain and joy.
I will not hesitate to go on singing this highest of truths!

1190

Oh human beings,
loosing your senses,
to which future do you head,
poisoning the air and sky,
transforming the earth into hell?

Claiming yourself superior to the animals, birds
and the growing plants,
your ego kisses the heights of the sky.

Can't you see the passage of time,
its shadow of destruction,
approaching rapidly to reverse your speed?

Destiny has declared you
as the most conscious of living beings:
with wisdom expansive like the sky,
move on, move on until the stars.

5004

Tender red leaves sprout on the tree branches.
Old leaves are blown away by spring storms.

The faded yellow leaves, dried and colourless,
have fallen neglected and lifeless like the dust.

Don't forget the fallen leaves.
Their stories should also be written:
through their history of light and shadow,
darkness can be removed.

NOTES

1. Anandamurti (1979) 'Mysticism and Yoga.'
2. -See Bhattacharya, (1999): 'In the lyrics of the Baúl, God is as illusive as the beloved, but attainable through the knowledge of one's self. His search, therefore, is not only for the Absolute, but also for the *Maner-Manush,* or 'the Man of the Heart', 'the Man within.'
-See also Anandamurti (1981) 'Rár´h-24': 'The spirit of Baul is: 'I am unable to embrace Him and make Him my own- Him whom I know, recognise and realise, and who is my nearest kin, my life and soul (in Rabindranath's words, Jiivan Devata)- and in a bid to embrace Him, I roam about, searching for Him vigorously in heaven, earth and the nether world.'
-'"Bandhu" is one who cannot bear separation, cannot live away. The bondage is so strong that they cannot live away. For this reason they are called "bandhu"... Is anybody a bandhu in this world? No, there is none. After death even the people who accompany you to the burning ground return to their respective homes once the cremation is over, they shall not go with you. Hence there is no bandhu in this world. There is only one bandhu, and he is Jagat-Bandhu.' (Anandamurti, 1978, 'Bandhu, Surhd, Mitrm and Sakha.)
3. A similar sentiment was expressed by Rabindranath Tagore on the purpose of beauty and harmony: 'The instruments of our necessity assert that we must have food, shelter, clothing, comforts and convenience. And yet men spend an immense amount of time in contradicting this assertion, to prove that they are not merely a catalogue of endless wants; that there is in them an ideal of perfection, a sense of unity, which is a harmony between parts and a harmony with surroundings.' (Tagore, 1922, 'The Poet's Religion.')
4. See Anandamurti, 1962, 'Ananda Sutram', Chapter 2, Sutra 8: 'Vis'aye Purus'ábhásah jiivátmá: The reflection of Purus'a in a unit object is called the jiivátmá (unit soul).'
5. -'For the eyes of those in whom a singular longing for

union with Brahma has awakened (Brahma praeti) this mundane world appears as the Brahma Loka, the Abode of Brahma- everything is He, everything is He.' (Anandamurti, 1956, 'This World and the Next.')

-'When the individual mind, in its unbounded love for God, merges its individual feeling of existence, all its sweet vibrations, all its rhythmic ideations, in the eternal bliss, in the Supreme Entity, and arrives, temporarily or permanently, at a state if mind without any samkalpa or vikalpa, this state of highest wisdom, the state of union with Supreme Cognition, is the state of turiiya. The state of turiiya is eternal bliss, and thus it has no external expression.' (Anandamurti, 1995, 'Namah Shivaya Shantaya.')

6. 'Now this sádhaná which is Sádhaná for complete merger, for unification, starts with fearful love. Love must be there. Unless and until there is love, there can be no unification. So love must be there but it starts with fearful love and ends in fearless love: and the space between fearful love and fearless love is the space of Sádhaná. What is Sádhaná? Sádhaná is the transformation of fearful love into fearless love.' (Anandamurti, 1964, 'The Stance of Salvation and how to Attain it.')

7. See Anandamurti, 1962, 'Ananda Sutram', Chapter 2, Sutra 14: 'Brahma satyam' jagadapi satymápeks'ikam: Brahma is absolute truth; the universe is also truth but relative.'

8. Anandamurti, 1967, 'Mantra Caetanya.'

9. Tagore, 1922.

10. -'A woman's path is the path of devotion, love and endurance. This does not mean that men cannot go on that path but that when a man wants to do so, his emotional state has to be that of a beloveds as was that of Chaetanya's or Rama Krishna Paramahansa. To become feminine has a spiritual meaning: it is to become receptive... if a man has to undertake the spiritual journey, he has to develop the woman within.' (Sharma, 2002, 'Exploring the Icons.')

-'The sharing of the feminine self is reflected in the many religious practices in which men and women seek to become female…' (Frazier, 2010).

11. 'But in fact, the Pandavas looked upon Kr's'na as their sakhá, their most intimate friend. Sakhya bháva is one of the different bhávas or relationships between the devotee and the Lord.' (Anandamurti, 1997, 'Parthasárathi Kr's'na and Sám'khya philosophy-2.')

12. A similar observation has been made regarding the differing Russian and American viewpoint regarding emotion: 'In the world of Dostoyevsky and other Russian writers of the nineteenth and twentieth centuries, moral and spiritual knowledge are achieved through intense and even violent feeling and suffering. This attitude continues to govern an important element of Russian intelligentsia even today. It accounts for what may seem otherwise peculiar comments by Aleksandr Solzhenitsyn at the Harvard commencement of 1978 when he complained about the lack of depth and character in the American personality. From the Russian perspective, the sober ethicality of many Americans, and their discomfort in the face of intense and violent feeling, make them appear pale and thin indeed.' (Leites, 1986, pg. 32).

13. Sepheri, 2013, pg.59.

14. Tagore, 2013, 'The Problem of Evil.'

15. Bhattacharya, 1999.

16. 'Many of mankind's primitive instincts (for example, the desire to kill and the insatiable craving for sexual gratification) are clearly harmful to the well-being of a human community. As a result civilisation creates laws that prohibit killing, rape, and adultery, and it implements severe punishments if such commandments are broken. This process, argues Freud, is an inherent quality of civilisation that instils perpetual feelings of discontent in its citizens. Freud's theme is that what works for civilisation doesn't necessarily work for man. Man, by nature aggressive and egoistical, seeks self-satisfaction.' (Freud, 2018.)

17. Sepheri, 2013, pg. 59.

18. See Murty, 2018.

19. - 'When the underlying spirit of humanism is extended to

everything, animate and inanimate, in this universe – I have designated this as "Neohumanism". This Neohumanism will elevate humanism to universalism, the cult of love for all created beings of this universe.' (Sarkar, 1999, 'Liberation of Intellect: Discourse 1.)

-'Neohumanism is a world-view characterised by love for the Supreme. In the early stages of developing one's spiritual devotion, the adoption of Neohumanistic principles – that is, abjuring all prejudices against other races, groups, religions, and less-evolved creatures – will safeguard and enhance the development of that devotion.

And once, in turn, a person comes to feel devotion for the Supreme, that devotion or love will ultimately overflow onto all objects created by the Supreme. One will come spontaneously to love all beings and objects as one loves the Supreme, free from any discrimination.

So devotion expands one's world-view, and the more expansive the world-view, the more one finds the ecstasy and peace of devotion.' (Sarkar, 1999, 'Neohumanism, Liberation of Intellect.'

BIBLIOGRAPHY

-Anandamurti, 1956, 'Subhasita Samgraha 4: This World and the Next.' Electronic Edition 2006.
-Anandamurti, 1962, 'Ananda Sutram.' Electronic Edition 2006.
-Anandamurti, 1964, 'Subhasita Samgraha 18: The stance of Salvation and How to Attain it.' Electronic Edition 2006.
-Anandamurti, 1967, 'Subhasita Samgraha 10: Mantra Caetanya.' Electronic Edition 2006.
-Anandamurti, 1978, 'Ananda Vacanamrtam 5: Bandhu, Suhrd, Mitram and Sakha.' Electronic Edition 2006.
-Anandamurti, 1979, 'Yoga Psychology: Mysticism and Yoga.' Electronic Edition 2006.
-Anandamurti, 1981, 'Rarh- The Cradle of Civilization.' Electronic Edition 2006.
-Anandamurti, 1995, 'Namah Shivaya Shantaya.' Kolkata: Ananda Marga Publications.
-Anandamurti, 1997, 'Namami Krsnasundaram.' Kolkata: Ananda Marga Publications.
-Bhattacharya, Deben. 1999. 'The Mirror of the Sky: Songs of the Baúls of Bengal.' Arizona: Hohm Press.
-Frazier, Jessica. 2010. 'New Topics in Feminist Religion: Becoming the Goddess.' Springer Science and Business Media.
-Freud, Sigmund. 2018. 'Civilization and its Discontents.' New Delhi: General Press. (E-Book).
-Leites, Edmund. 1986. 'The Puritan Conscience.' London: Yale University Press.
- Murty, GRK. 2014. 'India's Romance with Monsoon Rains.' IUP Journal of English Studies, September 2014.
-Sarkar, Prabhar Rainjan. 1999. 'Neohumanism: the Liberation of Intellect.' Kolkata: Ananda Marga Publications.
-Sepehri, Sohrab. 2013. 'A Selection of Poems from the Eight Books.' Bloomington, Baboa Press.
-Sharma, Kavita. 2002. 'Feminism, Tradition and Modernity: Exploring the Icons.' Indian Institute of Advanced Study.

-Tagore, Rabindranath. 1922. 'Creative Unity.' London: Macmillan and Co., Limited.
-Tagore, Rabindranath. 2013. 'Sádhana: The Realisation of Life.' Project Gutenberg Ebook.

www.ingramcontent.com/pod-product-compliance
Lightning Source LLC
Chambersburg PA
CBHW022018290426
44109CB00015B/1222